E S T A T E   P U B L

BARNSTAPLE

BIDEFORD BRAUNTON ILFRACOMBE N

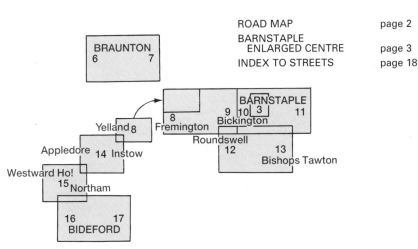

ROAD MAP	page 2
BARNSTAPLE ENLARGED CENTRE	page 3
INDEX TO STREETS	page 18

One-way Street	→
Car Park	🅿
Place of Worship	✚
Post Office	●
Public Convenience	Ⓒ
Pedestrianized	▨

Scale of street plans 4 inches to 1 mile
unless otherwise stated

Every effort has been made to verify the accuracy of information in this book but the publishers cannot accept responsibility for expense or loss caused by any error or omission. Information that will be of assistance to the user of the maps will be welcomed.

The representation of a road, track or footpath on the maps in this atlas is no evidence of the existence of a right of way.

Street plans prepared and published by ESTATE PUBLICATIONS, Bridewell House, TENTERDEN, KENT, and based upon the ORDNANCE SURVEY mapping with the permission of The Controller of H. M. Stationery Office.

The publishers acknowledge the co-operation of the local authorities of towns represented in this atlas.

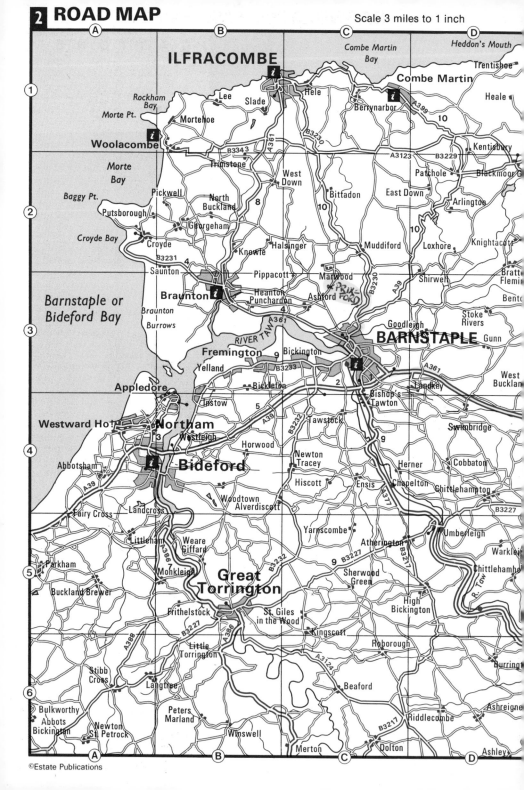

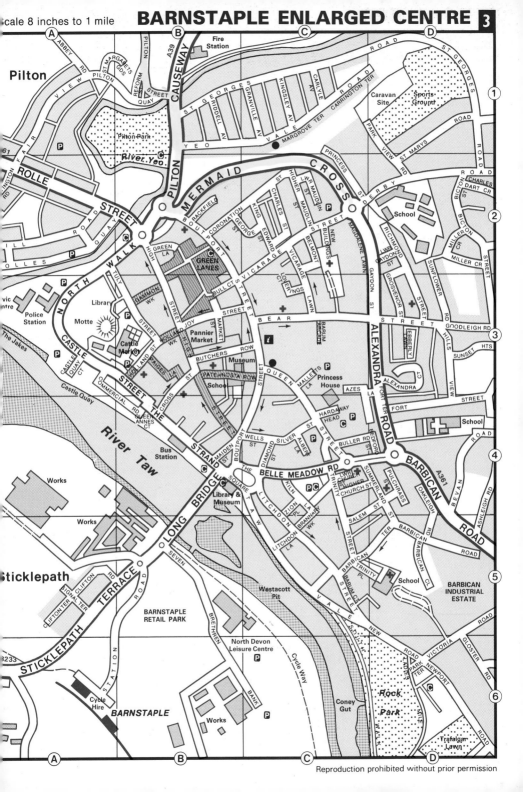

BARNSTAPLE ENLARGED CENTRE

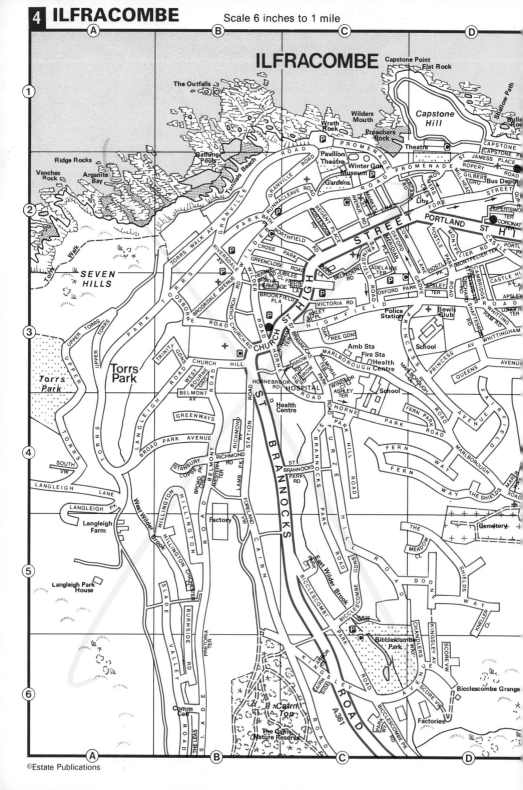

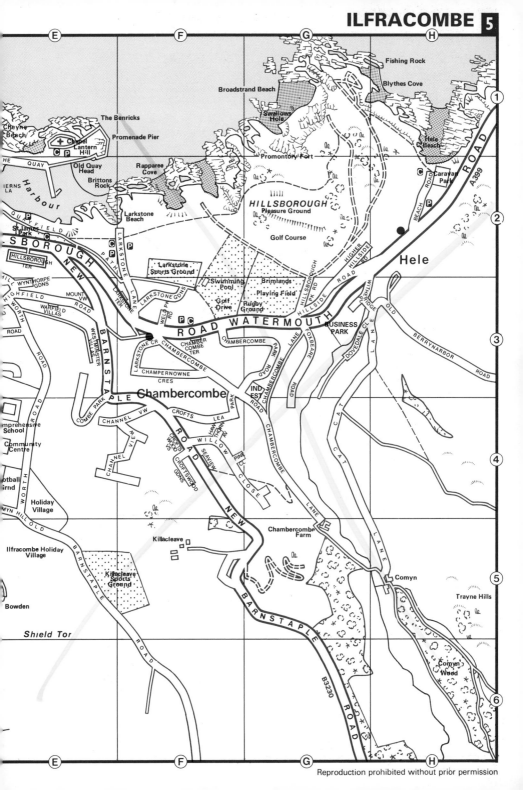

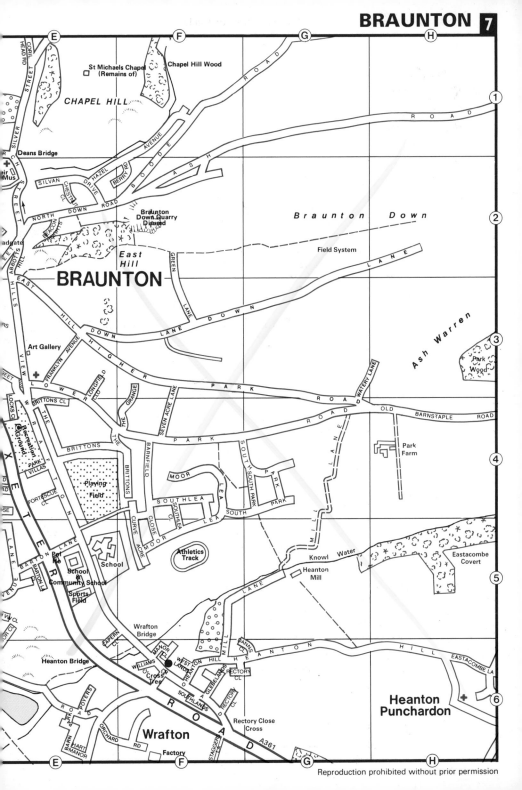

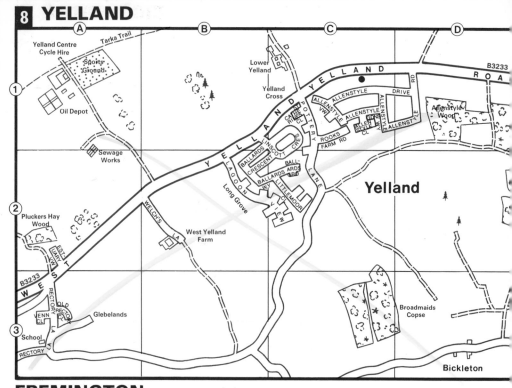

FREMINGTON

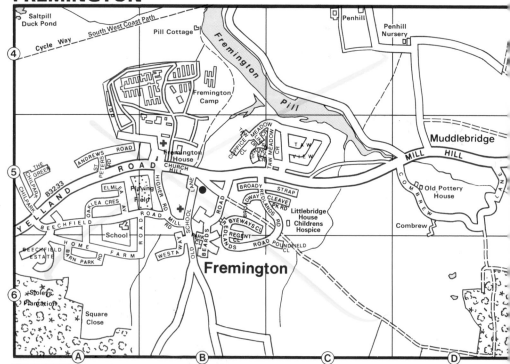

©Estate Publications

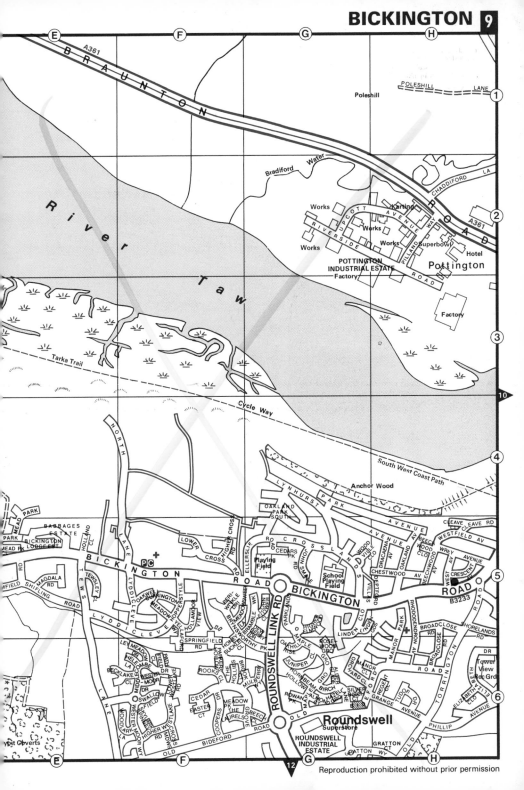

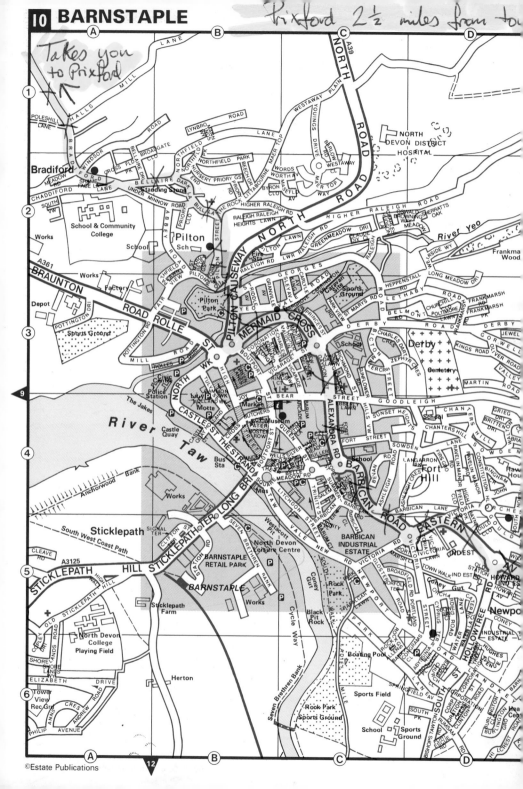

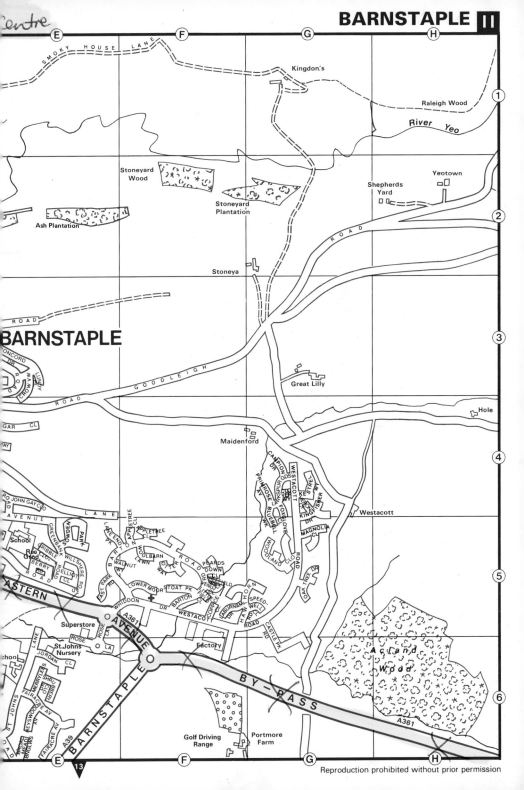

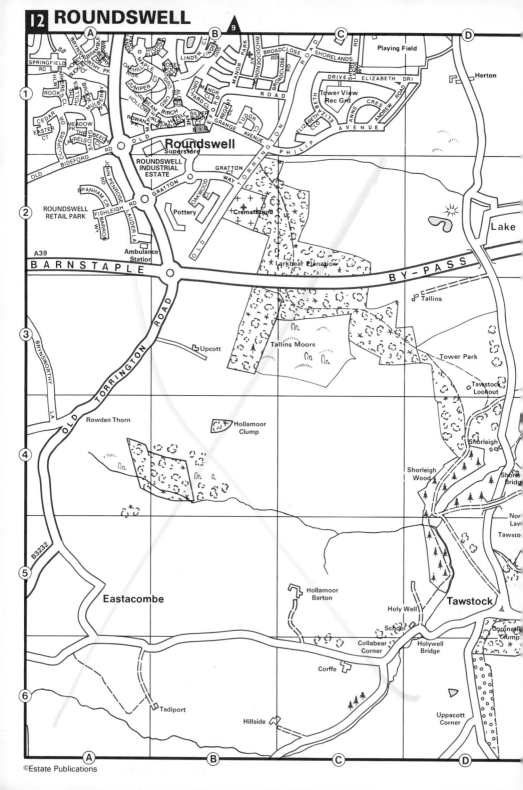

A   B   9   C   D

SPRINGFIELD RD

Herton

Playing Field

BROADCLOSE
SHORELANDS RD

Tower View Rec Grd
ELIZABETH DRIVE

ELIZABETH DRI
ANNS CRES
ANDREW ROAD
ELIZABETH CLO
AVENUE
PHILIP

CEDAR
EASTER CT
COOPERS RD
MEADOW PK
THE GROVE
BEECH
LAURELS DR
BIDEFORD
OLD

JOHN PENROSE RD
SPANHAM CR
FISHLEIGH RD
LAUDER LA
FIBARROW WY

Roundswell Superstore

ROUNDSWELL INDUSTRIAL ESTATE

GRATTON CT
GRATTON WAY

OLD TORRINGTON

MANOR PARK
LINDEN CL
RHODODENDRON RD
BROADCLOSE RD

MAPLE
OAK GRO
JUNIPER CT
HORNBEAM GRO
ROWAN
BIRCH
HAZEL
ELM
SILVER
ORCHARD CL
MANOR
REGENT
TUDOR
GRANGE AVENUE

Roundswell

ROUNDSWELL RETAIL PARK

Pottery
OAKWOOD

+ Crematorium

Ambulance Station

A39

BARNSTAPLE   BY-PASS

Lake

Tallins

Upcott

Tallins Moors

Tower Park

Tawstock Lookout

Rowden Thorn

Hollamoor Clump

Shorleigh

Shorleigh Wood

Shore Bridg

Nor Law

Tawsto

OLD TORRINGTON ROAD

BRYNSWORTHY LA

B3232

Eastacombe

Hollamoor Barton

Holy Well

School

Tawstock

Coronation Clump

Collabear Corner

Holywell Bridge

Corffe

Tadiport

Hillside

Uppacott Corner

1
2
3
4
5
6

©Estate Publications

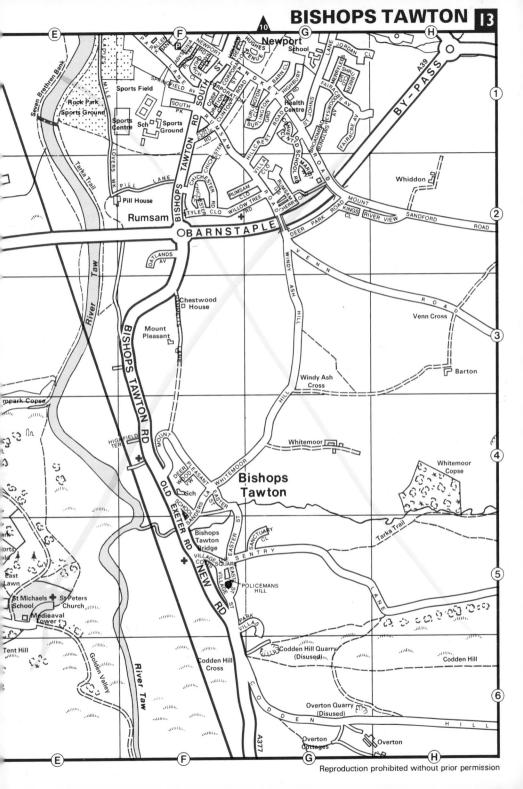

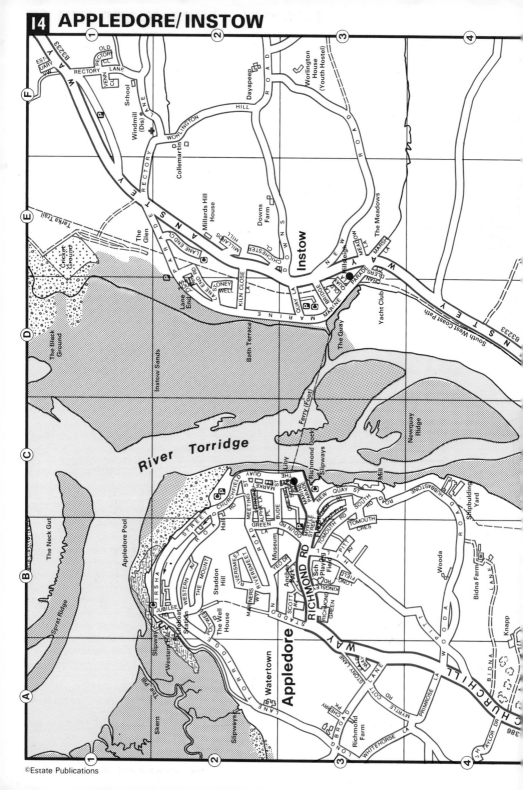

Instow

Appledore

River Torridge

Tarka Trail

South West Coast Path

Cricket Ground

The Black Ground

The Neck Gut

Appledore Pool

The Gut

Sprat Ridge

Newquay Ridge

Instow Sands

Beth Terrace

The Quay

Yacht Club

Ferry (Foot)

Richmond Dock

Slipways

Watertown

Wooda

Bidna Farm

Knapp

Shipbuilding Yard

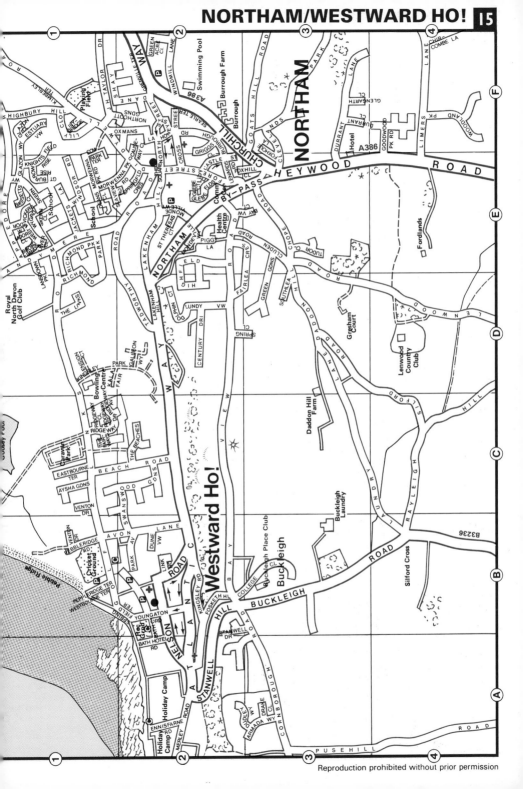

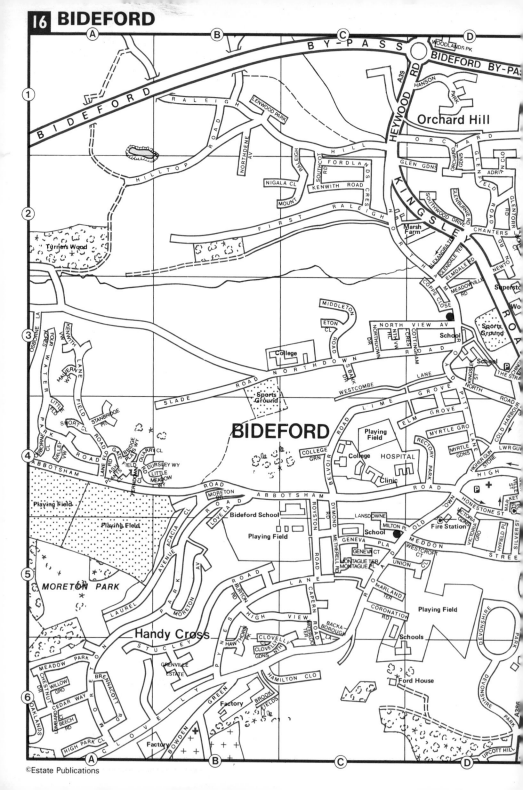

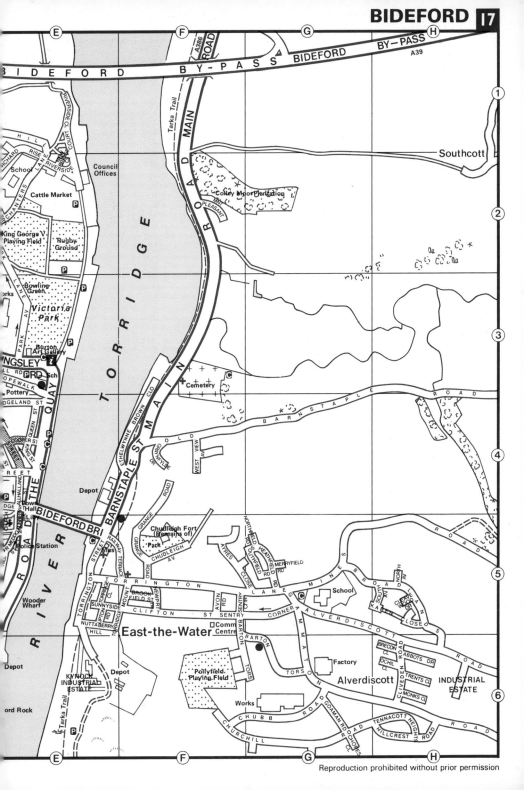

A - Z INDEX TO STREETS
with Postcodes

Peards Down Clo. EX32 11 F5
Periwinkle Dri. EX31 9 F5
Philip Av. EX31 12 B1
Pill La. EX32 13 F2
Pillard Way. EX31 9 G2
Pilton Causeway. EX32 3 B2
Pilton Lawn. EX31 10 B2
Pilton Quay. EX31 3 A1
Pilton St. EX31 3 B1
Poleshill La. EX31 9 H1
Policemans Hill. EX32 13 F5
Poltimore Lawn. EX32 10 D3
Port Marsh La. EX32 10 C5
Portland St. EX32 10 D5
Pottington Dri. EX31 10 A3
Pottington Rd. EX31 10 A3
Poundfield Clo. EX31 8 C6
Primrose Av. EX32 11 G4
Princess St. EX32 3 C1
Priory Gdns. EX31 10 B2
Priory Rd. EX31 10 B2
Proiry Clo. EX31 10 B2
Prospect Pl. EX32 10 D6
Pulchrass St. EX32 3 D4
Queen Annes Ct. EX31 3 B4
Queen St. EX32 3 C3
Rackfield. EX32 3 B2
Raleigh Heights. EX31 10 B2
Raleigh Lawn. EX31 10 B2
Raleigh Meadow. EX31 10 C2
Raleigh Rd. EX31 10 B2
Ravelin Manor Rd. EX32 10 D4
Redlands Rd. EX31 8 B5
Reform St. EX31 3 B1
Regent Clo
 Fremington. EX31 8 B6
Regent Clo
 Roundswell. EX31 9 H6
Rhododendron Av . EX31 9 H5
Richmond St. EX32 3 D2
Riddel Av. EX32 3 B1
River Vw. EX32 13 G2
Riverside Rd. EX31 9 G2
Rock Av. EX32 10 C6
Rock Gdns. EX32 10 C5
Rolle St. EX32 3 A2
Rolles Quay. EX31 3 A2
Rooks Clo. EX31 9 F6
Rose La. EX32 11 E5
Rosewood Gro. EX31 9 G6
Roundswell Link Rd.
 EX31 9 G6
Rowan Pk. EX31 9 G6
Rumsam Clo. EX32 13 F2
Rumsam Gdns. EX32 13 G2
Rumsam Rd. EX32 13 F1
St Georges Rd. EX32 3 B1
St Johns La. EX32 13 G1
St Margarets Gdns. EX31 3 A1
St Marys Rd. EX32 3 D2
St Peters Rd. EX31 8 A5
Salem St. EX32 3 C5
Sanctuary Clo. EX32 13 G5
Sanders La. EX32 13 F5
School La. EX32 13 F4
Sentry La. EX32 13 F5
Seven Brethren Bank.
 EX31 3 B5
Shame Face La. EX31 10 A2
Sherratts Oak. EX31 10 D2
Shifling Rd. EX31 9 E5
Shorelands Rd. EX32 10 A6
Shorelands Way. EX32 10 A6
Shrubbery Clo. EX32 13 G1
Signal Ter. EX31 3 A5
Silver Birch Ct. EX31 9 G6
Silver St. EX32 3 C4
Skylark Spinney. EX31 9 F6
Smoky House La. EX32 11 E1
South Grn. EX32 10 D5
South Park. EX32 10 D6
South St EX32 13 F1
South Vw. EX31 10 A2
South Wk. EX32 3 C5
Sowden La. EX32 10 C4
Sowden Pk. EX32 11 E5
Speedwell Clo. EX32 11 G5
Springfield Av. EX32 10 D6
Springfield Cres. EX31 8 B5
Springfield Rd. EX31 9 F6
Station Rd. EX31 3 A6
Sticklepath Hill. EX31 10 A5
Sticklepath Ter. EX31 3 A6
Stoat Pk. EX32 11 F5
Style Clo. EX32 13 F2
Summerland St. EX32 3 C4
Sunflower Clo. EX32 3 D2

Sunset Heights. EX32 3 D3
Swallowfield. EX31 9 F6
Taw Meadow Cres. EX31 8 C5
Taw Vale. EX32 3 C4
Taw Vw. EX31 8 C5
Tews La. EX31 9 E5
Tewsley Clo. EX31 9 E5
The Coombes. EX31 9 F6
The Green. EX31 8 A5
The Hollies. EX31 9 F6
The Laurels. EX31 9 F6
The Rock. EX31 10 B2
The Square,
 Barnstaple. EX32 3 B4
The Square
 Bishops Tawton. EX32 13 B4
The Strand. EX31 3 B4
Town Wk. EX32 10 D5
Trafalgar Lawn. EX32 10 D5
Treefield Wk. EX32 11 F5
Trinity Pl. EX32 3 C5
Trinity St. EX32 3 C4
Tudor Clo. EX31 12 B1
Tudor Dri. EX31 9 H6
Tuly St. EX31 3 A2
Under Minnow Rd.
 EX31 10 A2
Upcott Av. EX31 9 G2
Valley Clo. EX32 10 D3
Venlock Clo. EX32 11 F5
Venn Rd. EX32 13 G2
Vicarage Lawn. EX32 3 C2
Vicarage St. EX32 3 C2
Victoria Clo. EX32 10 D5
Victoria Lawn. EX32 10 D5
Victoria Rd. EX32 10 D5
Victoria St. EX32 10 D5
Villa Clo. EX32 13 G2
Village Cotts. EX32 13 F5
Village St. EX32 13 F5
Walnut Way. EX32 11 E5
Walton Way. EX32 10 D4
Water La. EX32 10 D6
Water Lane Clo. EX32 10 D6
Weirside Way. EX32 10 D2
Wells St. EX32 3 C4
West Av. EX31 9 H5
Westacott Rd. EX32 11 F5
Westaway. EX31 8 B6
Westaway Clo. EX31 10 C2
Westaway Plain. EX31 10 C1
Wester Moor Way. EX31 9 H5
Westfield Av. EX31 9 H5
Whiddon Dri. EX32 11 E5
Whitemoor Hill. EX32 13 F4
Wilkey Clo. EX32 10 D5
Willow Tree Rd. EX32 13 F2
Willshere Rd. EX32 11 E5
Windsor Rd. EX31 10 A2
Windy Ash La. EX32 13 G2
Woodland Clo. EX32 11 G5
Woodlark La. EX31 9 F6
Woodville Clo. EX31 9 G5
Woolbarn Lawn. EX32 11 F5
Wordsworth Av. EX31 10 B2
Wrey Av. EX31 9 H5
Yellaford Way. EX31 9 F5
Yelland Rd. EX31 8 A5
Yeo Vale Rd. EX32 3 B1
Youings Dri. EX31 10 C1
Zephyr Cres. EX31 10 C3
Zion Pl. EX32 3 C4

BIDEFORD

Abbots Dri. EX39 17 H6
Abbotsham Rd. EX39 16 A4
Acacia Clo. EX39 16 B5
Adrian Clo. EX39 16 D2
Alexandra Ter. EX39 17 E4
All Halland St. EX39 17 E4
Alverdiscott Rd. EX39 17 G5
Ash Plants Clo. EX39 16 A4
Avon Rd. EX39 17 F5
Ayres Clo. EX39 17 F5
Backaborough La. EX39 16 C5
Barton Tors. EX39 17 F5
Beech Rd. EX39 16 A6
Belvoir Rd. EX39 16 C4
Bideford Bridge. EX39 17 E4
Bideford By-Pass. EX39 16 A1
Bowden Grn. EX39 16 B6
Brecon Clo. EX39 17 H6
Brennacott Rd. EX39 16 A6
Bridge Plats Way. EX39 16 A4

Bridge St. EX39 17 E4
Bridgeland St. EX39 17 E4
Broadlands. EX39 17 G5
Brook Fields. EX39 16 B6
Brook Field St. EX39 17 F5
Burton Rd. EX39 16 B5
Bull Hill. EX39 16 B6
Buttgarden St. EX39 17 E5
Capern Rd. EX39 16 C5
Cedar Way. EX39 16 A6
Chanters La. EX39 16 D2
Chantry Av. EX39 17 E2
Chestnut Dri. EX39 16 A6
Chingswell St. EX39 16 D3
Chopes Clo. EX39 17 G6
Chubb Rd. EX39 17 F6
Chudleigh Av. EX39 17 F5
Church Wk. EX39 17 F6
Churchill Rd. EX39 17 F6
Cleave Wood Dri. EX39 17 H5
Clifton St. EX39 17 F5
Clivedon Rd. EX39 17 H6
Clovelly Clo. EX39 16 B6
Clovelly Gdns Nth. EX39 17 H6
Clovelly Rd. EX39 16 A6
Cold Harbour. EX39 16 D4
College Grn. EX39 16 C4
Cooper St. EX39 17 E4
Copps Clo. EX39 16 D3
Coronation Rd. EX39 16 C5
Cottingham Cres. EX39 16 D3
Devonshire Pk. EX39 16 D5
Dursley Way. EX39 16 A4
Dymond Rd. EX39 16 C4
Elm Gro. EX39 16 C4
Elmdale Rd. EX39 16 D3
Ethelwynne Brown Clo.
 EX39 17 F4
Eton Clo. EX39 16 D5
Ferndown Clo. EX39 16 A4
First Raleigh. EX39 16 B2
Fordlands Cres. EX39 16 A4
Four Acres. EX39 16 A3
Gammaton Rd. EX39 17 G5
Gate Field Rd. EX39 16 A4
Geneva Ct. EX39 16 C5
Geneva Pl. EX39 16 C5
Glen Gdns. EX39 16 C2
Glenburnie Rd. EX39 16 D2
Glendale Ter. EX39 16 D2
Glenfield Rd. EX39 16 D1
Glentorr Rd. EX39 16 D2
Goaman Rd. EX39 17 G6
Grange Rd. EX39 17 F5
Graynfylde Dri. EX39 17 F4
Grenville Est. EX39 16 B5
Grenville St. EX39 16 D4
Hamilton Clo. EX39 16 B6
Hawthorn Pk. EX39 16 B6
Heathfield Rd. EX39 17 G5
Heywood Rd. EX39 16 C1
High Pk Clo. EX39 16 A6
High St. EX39 16 D4
High Vw. EX39 16 B5
Higher Gun Stone. EX39 16 D4
Hillcrest Rd. EX39 17 H6
Hilltop Rd. EX39 16 A2
Honestone St. EX39 16 D4
Hyfield Pl. EX39 16 D5

INDUSTRIAL ESTATES
Kynock Ind. Est. EX39 17 E6
Karen Clo. EX39 17 H5
Kenwith Rd. EX39 16 C2
Kenwith Vw. EX39 16 A3
Kings St. EX39 17 E4
Kingsley Rd. EX39 16 C2
Kingsley Rd. EX39 16 E3
Lane Field Rd. EX39 16 A3
Lansdowne. EX39 16 A4
Laurel Av. EX39 16 A5
Lenwood Pk. EX39 16 B1
Lime Gro. EX39 16 A6
Little Field. EX39 16 A4
Little Mdw Way. EX39 16 A4
Lombard Clo. EX39 16 D4
Love La. EX39 16 B5
Lower Gun Stone. EX39 16 D4
Lower Meadow St. EX39 16 D4
Main Rd. EX39 17 F4
Malvern Way. EX39 16 A3
Market Pl. EX39 16 D4
Marland Ter. EX39 16 C5
Marlborough Ct. EX39 16 D4
Meadow Pk. EX39 16 A6
Meadowville Rd. EX39 16 D3
Meddon St. EX39 16 D4
Merryfield Rd. EX39 16 G5

Metherell Rd. EX39 16 C5
Middleton Rd. EX39 16 C3
Mill St. EX39 16 D4
Milton Pl. EX39 16 C5
Mines Rd. EX39 17 G5
Monks Clo. EX39 17 H6
Montague Pl. EX39 16 C5
Montague Ter. EX39 16 D4
Moreton Av. EX39 16 B5
Moreton Dri. EX39 16 B5
Moreton Park Rd. EX39 16 A6
Mount Pleasant. EX39 17 F2
Mount Raleigh. EX39 16 C2
Myrtle Gdns. EX39 16 D4
Myrtle Gro. EX39 16 D4
New Bridge Clo. EX39 17 E2
New Rd. EX39 16 D6
New St. EX39 17 E4
Newport Ter. EX39 17 F5
Newton Rd. EX39 16 D2
Nigala Clo. EX39 16 B2
North Av. EX39 17 H5
North Rd. EX39 16 D4
North View Av. EX39 16 C3
North View Hill. EX39 16 C3
Northam Rd. EX39 16 C2
Northdene Av. EX39 16 B2
Northdown Dri. EX39 16 C3
Northdown Rd. EX39 16 C3
Northfield Rd. EX39 17 G5
Nunnery Wk. EX39 17 E5
Nuttaberry Hill. EX39 17 E5
Oaklands. EX39 16 A6
Ochil Clo. EX39 17 H6
Old Barnstaple Rd. EX39 17 F4
Old Town EX39 16 D4
Orchard Gdns. EX39 16 D2
Orchard Hill. EX39 16 C1
Orchard Rise. EX39 17 E2
Osborne Clo. EX39 16 A4
Osborne La. EX39 16 A3
Park Av. EX39 17 E2
Park La. EX39 17 E2
Pill Rd. EX39 17 E3
Pitt La. EX39 16 D3
Pynes La. EX39 16 B6
Quarry Clo. EX39 16 A4
Queen St. EX39 17 E4
Railway Ter. EX39 17 E5
Raleigh Hill. EX39 16 B1
Rectory Pk. EX39 16 D4
Riverside Clo. EX39 17 E1
Riverside Ct. EX39 17 E2
Ropewalk. EX39 17 E3
Royston Rd. EX39 16 C4
Sentry Corner. EX39 17 F5
Short Clo. EX39 16 A4
Silver St. EX39 16 D5
Slade Rd. EX39 16 B4
South Av. EX39 17 H5
South Bank Dri. EX39 16 C3
Southcot Rd. EX39 16 C4
Southfield Rd. EX39 17 G5
Southwood Dri. EX39 16 D2
Stanbridge Pk. EX39 16 A4
Stucley Rd. EX39 16 A6
Sunnyside. EX39 17 E5
Tennacott Heights. EX39 17 H6
The Quay. EX39 17 E4
The Strand. EX39 16 D3
Torridge Clo. EX39 17 E5
Torridge Hill. EX39 17 D5
Torridge Mount. EX39 17 E5
Torrington La. EX39 17 E5
Torrington St. EX39 17 E5
Trents Clo. EX39 17 H6
Union Clo. EX39 16 C5
Upcott Hill. EX39 16 D6
Upton Rd. EX39 17 E5
Valley Vw. EX39 16 A4
Victoria Gdns. EX39 16 A6
Victoria Gro. EX39 16 D5
Water Park Rd. EX39 16 A5
Waterloo Ter. EX39 16 C5
West View Av. EX39 17 F4
Westacombe La. EX39 16 C3
Westcroft Ct. EX39 16 B6
Willow Clo. EX39 16 A6
Woodlands Pk. EX39 16 D1

BRAUNTON

Abbots Hill. EX33 7 E2
Arlington Ter. EX33 6 D4
Ash Rd. EX33 7 F2

Ashmead Gro. EX33 6 C3
Ashton Cres. EX33 6 C4
Barn Pk. EX33 7 E6
Barnfield Clo. EX33 7 F4
Barton Av. EX33 6 D5
Barton Clo. EX33 6 D5
Barton Lane Clo. EX33 7 E5
Beacon Heights. EX33 7 E2
Beech Gro. EX33 6 B2
Berry Rd. EX33 7 E2
Bias La. EX33 6 D3
Boode Rd. EX33 7 F2
Brittons Clo. EX33 7 E4
Broadgate. EX33 6 D2
Brookfield Clo. EX33 6 D4
Burrows Clo. EX33 6 C4
Burrows Pk. EX33 6 C3
Butts Path. EX33 6 D2
Caen Field. EX33 6 D3
Caen Gdns. EX33 6 D3
Caen St. EX33 6 D3
Capern Clo. EX33 7 E6
Cavie Cres. EX33 6 A2
Chaloners Rd. EX33 6 D1
Chapel St. EX33 6 D3
Chestnut Clo. EX33 7 E2
Chichesters Yd. EX33 6 D4
Church St. EX33 6 D1
Colley Park Rd. EX33 6 D4
Coril Head Rd. EX33 7 E1
Curve Acre. EX33 7 F4
Danns Clo. EX33 7 F6
Davids Clo. EX33 6 D4
Down Clo. EX33 7 E3
Dune View Rd. EX33 6 B2
Dyers Clo. EX33 7 E3
East Hill. EX33 7 E3
East Meadow Rd. EX33 6 A1
East St. EX33 6 D3
Eastacombe La. EX33 7 F6
Exeter Rd. EX33 7 E4
Fairlynch Clo. EX33 6 A1
Fairlynch Gro. EX33 6 B1
Fairlynch La. EX33 6 A1
Field Clo. EX33 6 C4
Field La. EX33 6 C4
Fortescue Clo. EX33 7 E4
Frankyln Av. EX33 7 E3
Frog La. EX33 6 D2
Galloway La. EX33 6 C6
Garden Clo. EX33 6 B2
Glebelands. EX33 7 F6
Goodgates Clo. EX33 6 B2
Goodgates Cres. EX33 6 B2
Goodgates Gro. EX33 6 B2
Goodgates Pk. EX33 6 B2
Goodgates Rd. EX33 6 B2
Great Field Gdns. EX33 6 C3
Green La. EX33 7 F2
Greenacre. EX33 6 B2
Gubbins La. EX33 6 D4
Hart Manor. EX33 7 E6
Hazel Av. EX33 7 E2
Heanton Hill. EX33 7 F6
Heanton St. EX33 6 D3
Higher Park Rd. EX33 7 E3
Hills Vw. EX33 7 E3
Homer Cres. EX33 6 A1
Homer Dri. EX33 6 B1
Homer Rd. EX33 6 A1
Irving Clo. EX33 6 A2
Kingsacre. EX33 6 B3
Limtree Gro. EX33 6 B3
Linden Clo. EX33 6 D2
Locks Clo. EX33 7 E3
Longfield Clo. EX33 7 E3
Lower Cleve. EX33 6 C2
Lower Park Rd. EX33 7 E3
Manor Clo. EX33 7 F6
Mill La. EX33 7 F6
Mill Stile. EX33 6 C4
Mint Park Rd. EX33 6 A1
Moor La. EX33 6 A3
Moor Lea. EX33 7 F4
Mowstead Rd. EX33 6 A2
North Down Rd. EX33 7 E2
North St. EX33 6 D3
Old Barnstaple Rd. EX33 7 F6
Orchard Clo. EX33 6 C3
Orchard Rd. EX33 7 E6
Palmers Clo. EX33 6 D4
Park Vs. EX33 7 E4
Pill Gdns. EX33 6 D5
Pixie Dell. EX33 6 B2
Pixie La. EX33 6 B2
Poyers. EX33 7 E6
Quantocks. EX33 6 B3

→ This is not South View, PRIXFORD.

Ralph Rd. EX33 6 A2
Rectory Clo. EX33 7 F6
Rock Hill. EX33 6 D2
Sage Park Rd. EX33 6 A1
St Brannocks Well Clo.
  EX33 6 D1
Saunton Clo. EX33 6 C3
Saunton Rd. EX33 6 A2
Scurfield. EX33 6 D2
Scurfield Clo. EX33 6 D2
Second Field La. EX33 6 C3
Seven Acre La. EX33 7 F4
Sharlands La. EX33 6 C3
Shortcombe Dri. EX33 6 A1
Silver St. EX33 7 E1
Sings La. EX33 6 D3
Skir. EX33 6 D2
South Pk. EX33 7 F4
South St. EX33 6 D5
South View Clo. EX33 7 E5
Southlands. EX33 7 F6
Southlea. EX33 7 F4
Southlea Clo. EX33 7 F4
Staddon Clo. EX33 6 C3
Staggers La. EX33 7 F6
Stallards. EX33 6 B2
Station Rd. EX33 6 D4
The Brittons. EX33 7 E4
The Fairway. EX33 6 A2
The Grange. EX33 7 F4
The Moorings. EX33 6 D2
The Square. EX33 6 D3
Town Farm Ct. EX33 6 C3
Towns End. EX33 6 C3
Velator Clo. EX33 7 E5
Velator Dri. EX33 6 D6
Velator Lane Av. EX33 6 D4
Velator Rd. EX33 6 D6
Watery La. EX33 7 G3
Wellclose Rd. EX33 6 D4
West Cross. EX33 6 D3
West Hill La. EX33 6 C2
West Land. EX33 7 E4
West Meadow Clo. EX33 6 A2
West Meadow Rd. EX33 6 A2
West Park. EX33 6 C2
Westmead Clo. EX33 6 C3
Willand Rd. EX33 6 C2
Williams Clo. EX33 7 F6
Willoway Gro. EX33 6 C3
Willoway La. EX33 6 B1
Willoways Clo. EX33 6 C2
Willowfield. EX33 6 C1
Wrafton Rd. EX33 7 E4

ILFRACOMBE

Adelaide Ter. EX34 4 C2
Apsley Ter. EX34 4 D3
Apsley Vs. EX34 4 D3
Arbor Clo. EX34 4 C6
Arcade Rd. EX34 4 C2
Ashley Ter. EX34 4 C3
Avenue Rd. EX34 4 C2
Balmoral Ter. EX34 4 C3
Bath Pl. EX34 4 B2
Beach Rd. EX34 5 H2
Belmont Av. EX34 4 B3
Belmont Rd. EX34 4 B4
Belvedere Rd. EX34 4 C2
Berkley Pl. EX34 4 B2
Bicclescombe Gdns. EX34 4 C5
Bicclescombe Pk Rd. EX34 4 C5
Broad Park Av. EX34 4 A4
Broad Park Cres. EX34 4 B4
Broad St. EX34 4 D2
Brookdale Av. EX34 4 B3
*Brookfield Cotts,
  Friendship La. EX34 4 C3
Brookfield Pl. EX34 4 B3
Burnside Rd. EX34 4 B5

Burrow Rd. EX34 4 C3
Cairn Rd. EX34 4 B4
Cairn Side. EX34 4 C6
Cambridge Gro. EX34 4 D2
Capstone La. EX34 4 D1
Capstone Rd. EX34 4 D1
Castle Hill. EX34 4 D3
Castle Hill Av. EX34 4 D3
Castle Ter. EX34 4 D3
Cat La. EX34 5 H3
Chambercombe Cres.
  EX34 5 F3
Chambercombe La. EX34 5 G4
Chambercombe Park Rd.
  EX34 5 F3
Chambercombe Ter. EX34 5 F3
Chandlers Way. EX34 5 F4
Chanel Vw. EX34 5 E4
Chichester Clo. EX34 4 B5
Church Hill. EX34 4 D3
Church Rd. EX34 4 B4
Church St. EX34 4 B3
*Clifton Ct,
  Friendship La. EX34 4 C3
Combe Pk. EX34 5 E4
Comyn Hill. EX34 5 E4
Coronation Ter. EX34 4 D2
Cow La. EX34 4 C2
Crofts Lea Pk. EX34 5 E3
Croftswood Gdns. EX34 5 F4
Croftswood Vs. EX34 5 F4
Cross Pk. EX34 4 B2
Doone Way. EX34 4 D5
Dovedale Clo. EX34 5 G3
Fairfield. EX34 4 D3
Fern Pk. EX34 4 C4
Fern Way. EX34 4 C4
Fore St. EX34 4 D2
Foreland View. EX34 4 B5
Fortesque Rd. EX34 4 C2
Foxbeare Rd. EX34 5 G3
Friendship La. EX34 4 C3
Furle Hill Rd. EX34 4 C4
Gilbert Gro. EX34 4 D2
Granville Rd. EX34 4 B2
Greenclose Rd. EX34 4 B2
Greenways. EX34 4 B4
Hawthorn Av. EX34 5 F4
Hermitage Rd. EX34 4 B2
High Street. EX34 4 C2
Higher Hillside Rd. EX34 5 G2
Highfield Rd. EX34 4 B4
Highfield Ter. EX34 5 E3
Hillborough Rd. EX34 4 D2
Hillington. EX34 4 B5
Hillsborough Pk Rd. EX34 5 G3
Hillsborough Ter. EX34 5 E2
Hillside Rd. EX34 5 G3
Horne Park Rd. EX34 4 B4
Horne Rd. EX34 4 B3
Hornebrook Av. EX34 4 B4
Hostle Pk. EX34 4 D2
Hostle Park Rd. EX34 4 D2
Jubilee Clo. EX34 4 C3
Kingsley Av. EX34 4 C6
Kneller Clo. EX34 4 D5
Lamb Pk. EX34 4 B4
Langleigh La. EX34 4 A4
Langleigh Pk. EX34 4 A4
Langleigh Rd. EX34 4 A4
Larkstone Cres. EX34 5 F3
Larkstone Gdns. EX34 5 F3
Larkstone La. EX34 5 F3
Larkstone Ter. EX34 5 E3
Longfield Ter. EX34 4 D3
Market St. EX34 4 C2
Marlborough Clo. EX34 4 D3
Marlborough Rd. EX34 4 C3
Marlborough Way. EX34 4 D4
Meadow Clo. EX34 4 D5
Meridian Pl. EX34 4 C2
Mill Head. EX34 4 D2
Montpelier Rd. EX34 4 D2

Montpelier Ter. EX34 4 D2
Mount View. EX34 5 E3
*Neva Cotts,
  Friendship La. EX34 4 C3
New Barnstaple Rd. EX34 5 E2
Northfield Rd. EX34 4 B2
Oaktree Gdns. EX34 4 C3
Old Barnstaple Rd. EX34 5 E5
Old Berrynarbor Rd.
  EX34 5 G3
Orchard Rd. EX34 4 D3
Osborne Rd. EX34 4 B3
Oxford Gro. EX34 4 C2
Oxford Pk. EX34 4 C3
Park Ct. EX34 4 C5
Park Hill Rd. EX34 4 C4
Park Way. EX34 4 C6
Pine Clo. EX34 5 F4
Portland Pk. EX34 4 D2
Portland St. EX34 4 D2
Pretoria Ter. EX34 4 B6
Princes Av. EX34 4 D3
Promenade. EX34 4 C1
Quayfield Path. EX34 5 E2
Quayfield Rd. EX34 4 D2
Queens Av. EX34 4 D3
Regent Pl. EX34 4 C2
Richmond Av. EX34 4 B4
Richmond Rd. EX34 4 B4
Riversdale Rd. EX34 4 B2
Ropery Rd. EX34 4 D2
Runnacleave Rd. EX34 4 C2
Rupertswood Ter. EX34 4 D2
St Brannocks Pk Rd.
  EX34 4 C3
St Brannocks Rd EX34 4 B4
St James Pl. EX34 4 B2
St Peters Ter. EX34 4 D2
Score Vw. EX34 4 D6
Seaview. EX34 5 F4
Shaftesbury Rd. EX34 4 D3
Slade Rd. EX34 4 B6
Slade Valley Rd. EX34 4 B5
Sommers Cres. EX34 4 D2
South Burrow Rd. EX34 4 C3
South Vw. EX34 4 A4
Springfield Rd. EX34 4 C2
Stanbury Copse. EX34 4 B4
Station Rd. EX34 4 B4
Tarry La. EX34 4 C2
The Hermitage. EX34 4 B3
The Lanes. EX34 4 C2
The Leas. EX34 4 B6
The Quay. EX34 4 D2
The Shields. EX34 4 D4
Torrs Pk. EX34 4 A4
Torrs Walk Av. EX34 4 B2
Trinity Gdns. EX34 4 B3
Upper Torrs. EX34 4 A3
Victoria Rd. EX34 4 D3
Warfield Vs. EX34 5 E3
Watermouth Rd. EX34 5 F3
Weld Park Rd. EX34 5 F3
Westbourne Gro. EX34 4 B3
Western Ter. EX34 4 B4
Westminster Vs. EX34 5 E3
Whiteridge Pl. EX34 5 G3
Whittingham Rd. EX34 4 B2
Wilder Rd. EX34 4 B2
Willow Clo. EX34 5 F4
Windsor Ct. EX34 4 C3
Winsham Ter. EX34 4 B3
Worth Rd. EX34 5 E3
Wynthorpe Gdns. EX34 5 E2

NORTHAM/ WESTWARD HO!

Appledore Rd. EX39 15 E1
Armada Way. EX39 15 A3
Atlantic Way. EX39 15 A2

Avon. La. EX39 15 B1
Aysha Gdns. EX39 15 C1
Bassetts Clo. EX39 15 E1
Bath Ct. EX39 15 B2
Bath Hotel Rd. EX39 15 A2
Bay View Ct. EX39 15 E3
Bay View Rd. EX39 15 C1
Beach Rd. EX39 15 C1
Broadlands. EX39 15 E1
Buckleigh Rd. EX39 15 B3
Burrough Rd. EX39 15 E2
Castle St. EX39 15 E2
Causeway Clo. EX39 15 E1
Century Dri. EX39 15 D2
Chircombe La. EX39 15 F4
Chope Rd. EX9 15 E3
Churchill Way. EX39 15 E3
Clevelands Pk. EX39 15 E3
Cluden Rd. EX39 15 B2
College Clo. EX39 15 B2
Cornborough Rd. EX39 15 A3
Cow Park Ter. EX39 15 E1
Cross St. EX39 15 E2
Daddon Hill. EX39 15 D3
Dane Shay. EX39 15 F2
Deans Clo. EX39 15 E1
Diddywell Rd. EX39 15 E1
Dolphin Ct. EX39 15 E3
Drake Clo. EX39 15 A3
Dudley Way. EX39 15 A3
Dune View. EX39 15 B2
Durrant Clo. EX39 15 F3
Durrant La. EX39 15 E3
Eastbourne Ter. EX39 15 C1
Ennisfarne Rd. EX39 15 A2
Ensign Ct. EX39 15 D1
Estuary View. EX39 15 F1
Fairlea Cres. EX39 15 D2
Fore St. EX39 15 E2
Fosketh Hill. EX39 15 B2
Foxhill Clo. EX39 15 E2
Foxhole La. EX39 15 E3
Galleon Way. EX39 15 D1
Glazon Clo. EX39 15 F1
Glazon Way. EX39 15 F1
Glebe Ct. EX39 15 E2
Glebe Flds. EX39 15 E2
Glengarth Co. EX39 15 F3
Goats Hill Rd. EX39 15 F3
Golf Links Rd. EX39 15 B1
Goodwood Pk Rd. EX39 15 F3
Great Burrow Rise. EX39 15 E1
Green Acre Clo. EX39 15 F2
Green Gdns. EX39 15 D3
Grenville Ter. EX39 15 E1
Griggs Clo. EX39 15 F2
Heywood Rd. EX39 15 E3
Highbury Hill. EX39 15 E3
Highfield. EX39 15 D2
Honey St. EX39 15 E2
J H Taylor Dri. EX39 15 F1
Jackets La. EX39 15 D1
Kala Fair. EX39 15 D1
Kimberley Ter. EX39 15 F1
Kingsley Pk. EX39 15 D1
Kingsley Rd. EX39 15 B2
Knights Field Rise. EX39 15 E1
Lakenham Hill. EX39 15 D2
Lansdown Pk. EX39 15 E1
Laundry La. EX39 15 B4
Lenards Rd. EX39 15 E2
Lenwood Rd. EX39 15 D3
Lever Clo. EX39 15 E1
Lily Clo. EX39 15 F1
Lilybridge. EX39 15 F1
Limers La. EX39 15 E4
Link Rd. EX39 15 D2
Lundy Vw. EX39 15 D2
Merlay Rd. EX39 15 A2
Mondeville Way. EX39 15 E1
Morwenna Pk Rd. EX39 15 E1
Nelson Rd. EX39 15 A2
North St. EX39 15 E2

Northam By-Pass. EX39 15 E2
Northcotts Gdns. EX39 15 F2
Oxmans La. EX39 15 F1
Park Av. EX39 15 B2
Pepperidge Rd. EX39 15 B1
Pepperidge Ter. EX39 15 B1
Piggy La. EX39 15 B1
Pusehill Rd. EX39 15 A3
Rayleigh Hill. EX39 15 B4
Richmond Pk. EX39 15 D1
Ridgeway Av. EX39 15 C1
Ridgeway Clo. EX39 15 C1
Ridgeway Ct. EX39 15 C1
Ridgeway Dri. EX39 15 C1
St Theresas Ct. EX39 15 E2
Sandymere Rd. EX39 15 D1
Sea View Rd. EX39 15 E2
Searle Ter. EX39 15 F2
Silford Rd. EX39 15 C4
Skern Clo. EX39 15 E1
Skern Way. EX39 15 E1
Southlea. EX39 15 D3
Springfield Cres. EX39 15 E2
Springfield Ter. EX39 15 B2
Stanwell Dri. EX39 15 B2
Stanwell Hill. EX39 15 A2
Swanswood Gdns. EX39 15 B3
Tadworth Rd. EX39 15 D2
The Beaches. EX39 15 C1
The Fairways. EX39 15 C1
The Links. EX39 15 D1
The Square. EX39 15 E2
Tudor Clo. EX9 15 E3
Venton Dri. EX39 15 B1
Venton Dri. EX39 15 B1
Vickers Ground. EX39 15 E1
West Moor Clo. EX39 15 E1
West Moor Way. EX39 15 E1
Westbourne Ter. EX39 15 B1
Windmill La. EX39 15 F2
Windsor Rd. EX39 15 E1
Woodland Park. EX39 15 F4
Youngaton Rd. EX39 15 B2

YELLAND

Allenstyle Clo. EX31 8 C1
Allenstyle Dri. EX31 8 C1
Allenstyle Gdns. EX31 8 C1
Allenstyle Rd. EX31 8 C1
Allenstyle Vw. EX31 8 C1
Allenstyle Way. EX31 8 C1
Ballards Cres. EX31 8 B2
Ballards Gro. EX31 8 C2
Ballards Way. EX31 8 B2
Estuary Vw. EX31 8 A2
Lagoon Vw. EX31 8 B2
Linscott Cres. EX31 8 B1
Littlemoor Clo. EX31 8 C2
Old Rectory Clo. EX39 8 A3
Pottery La. EX31 8 C1
Rectory La. EX31 8 A3
Rooks Farm Rd. EX31 8 C1
St Catherines Clo. EX31 8 C1
Venn Clo. EX31 8 A3
Welch's La. EX31 8 B2
West Yelland. EX31 8 A3
Yelland Rd. EX31 8 C1